dabble lab

10-MINUTE
YARN
PROJECTS

BY SARAH L. SCHUETTE

CAPSTONE PRESS
a capstone imprint

Dabble Lab is published by Capstone Press, a Capstone imprint.
1710 Roe Crest Drive, North Mankato, Minnesota 56003
www.capstonepub.com

Library of Congress Cataloging-in-Publication data is available on the Library of Congress website.
ISBN 978-1-5435-9097-5 (library binding)
ISBN 978-1-5435-9103-3 (eBook PDF)

Summary: Got extra yarn in your makerspace? Put that yarn to use with some quick and easy makerspace projects. From dolls and animals to plant holders and dragon eggs, these 10-minute yarn projects will have kids making in no time!

Editorial Credits
Editor: Shelly Lyons; Designer: Tracy McCabe;
Media Researcher: Tracy Cummins; Production Specialist: Katy LaVigne;
Project Production: Marcy Morin

Photo Credits
All photographs by Capstone: Karon Dubke

Design Elements
Shutterstock: ArtMari, balabolka, BewWanchai, Bjoern Wylezich, Golden Shrimp, HNK, Jenov Jenovallen, Koritsia, Milya, nichy, Olha Yerofieieva, Ortis, Pacharawi Imsuwan, Tukang Desain, Vintage Love Story

All internet sites appearing in back matter were available and accurate when this book was sent to press.

Printed and bound in China. 5486

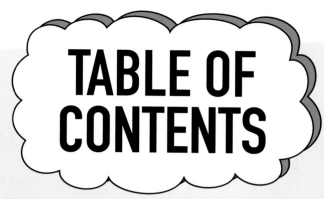

TABLE OF CONTENTS

GOT 10 MINUTES?

Do you have 10 minutes? Grab some yarn and make the most of that time by creating a cool new bracelet, cell phone holder, or bookmark. These quick and easy projects will inspire you.

General Supplies and Tools

aluminum foil

cardboard

craft sticks

glue (quick-drying)/low-temperature
  hot glue

recycled lids, bottles, cans, cups

scissors

toothpicks

yarn

Tips

- Before starting a project, gather the supplies and tools needed.

- When weaving or wrapping something larger in yarn, leave the yarn attached to the ball to make sure you have enough.

- If you cut the yarn too short to finish a project, tie on another piece and keep going.

- Ask an adult to help you with sharp tools.

- Change things up! Don't be afraid to make these projects your own.

POM-POM, PLEASE!

Pom-poms are simple and easy to make. Experiment with different shapes and colors. The possibilities are endless!

What You Need:

scissors
yarn
googly eyes
pipe cleaners
fork/cardboard (optional)

What You Do:

1 Cut a piece of yarn as long as your hand. Lay it between your two middle fingers.

2 Wrap more yarn loosely around the outside of your hand, about 20 times.

3 With your free hand, loosely tie the piece of yarn that's between your fingers around the wrapped yarn.

4 Slip the wrapped yarn off your hand and pull the yarn tie tight. Double knot it.

5 Cut the two yarn loops in half and trim your pom-pom.

6 To make animals, use short pieces of yarn to tie pom-poms together. Add googly eyes and pipe cleaners for feelers/horns.

TIP To make a smaller pom-pom, use a fork instead of your hand. You can also wrap yarn around a piece of cardboard.

SMILE AND BE HAPPY DOLL

Want to make someone smile? Make this simple
stick doll and give it as a gift. Clip it to a
friend's backpack or put it in a locker
to remind someone to smile.

What You Need:

yarn

large hole beads

scissors

quick-drying glue

stick

fabric pieces

craft magnet or
   clothespin (optional)

marker (optional)

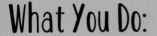

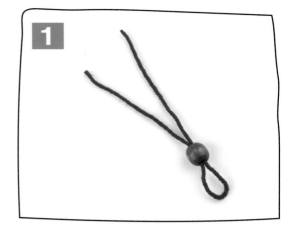

What You Do:

1 Cut a piece of yarn as long as your hand. Fold it in half and thread the loop through the hole of a bead.

2 Tie the loop of yarn in a knot, tight up against the bead. The loop should be long enough to look like hair. Cut the loop in half and pull apart the strands to create "hair".

3 Glue the end of the bead without the knot to the top of a small stick. Wrap the two yarn strands around the top end of the stick to look like a neck.

4 Glue fabric pieces to the stick to look like clothes. Add yarn pieces for extra decoration.

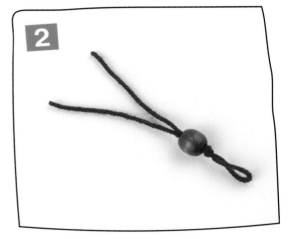

TIP Glue a craft magnet or clothespin to the back of the doll. Add faces with a marker, if you wish.

9

YARN ANIMAL

Go wild! Use your imagination and shape foil into
any animal you can think of. How about
a hummingbird? Perhaps you like octopuses?
Pick one and get making!

What You Need:

foil
yarn
scissors
cardboard
toothpicks
quick-drying glue (optional)

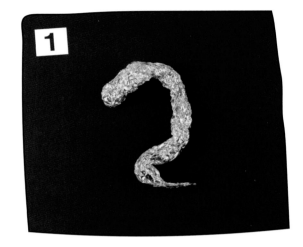

What You Do:

1 Shape foil into an animal shape.

2 Wrap the foil in yarn.

3 Use cardboard and toothpicks to add details like wings and beaks.

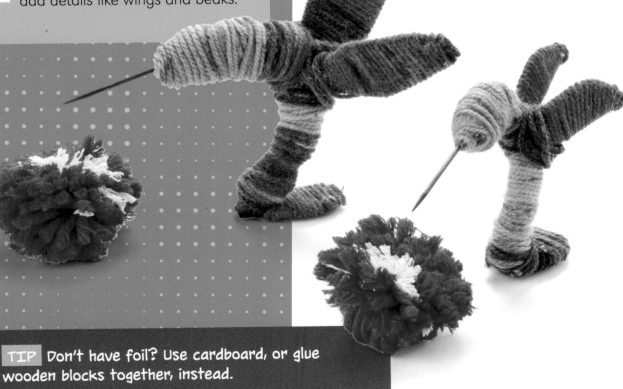

TIP Don't have foil? Use cardboard, or glue wooden blocks together, instead.

11

CELL PHONE STAND

Know someone who could use a cell phone stand? Check out this simple project you can make in minutes. Leave it on someone's desk as a fun surprise!

What You Need:

7-8 craft sticks
tape/quick-drying glue
yarn
cardboard (optional)

What You Do:

1 Lay two craft sticks together in an upside down V-shape. Tape or glue the sticks together where they meet.

2 Glue a third stick to the point of the V, so the V stands up.

3 Glue three or four other craft sticks together at the edges to create a flat surface. Then glue one edge to the center of the upside down V, to form a shelf.

4 Wrap the stand in yarn.

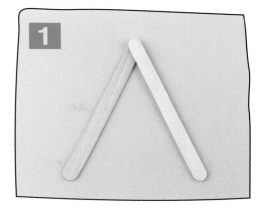

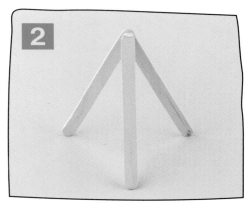

TIP Cut any shape you'd like out of cardboard, the same size as a phone. Glue one craft stick to the back so it stands up. Wrap the shape in yarn. Set a phone against this holder for another option.

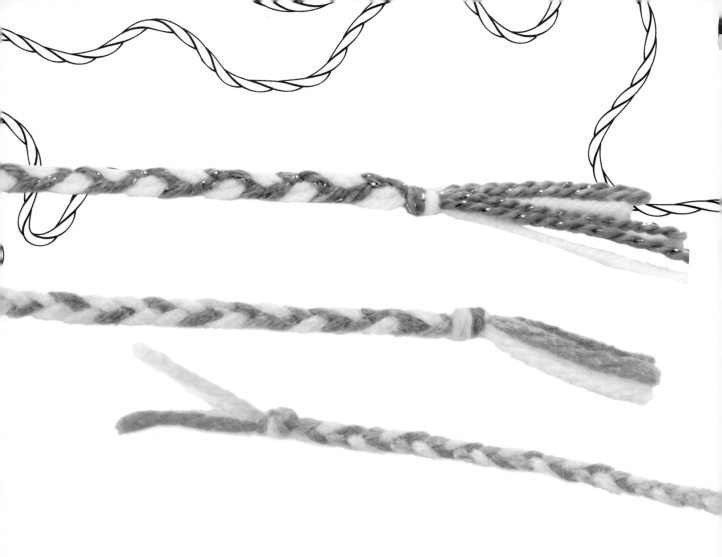

BRAIDING

Whether you already know how to braid, or you just want to learn, these friendship bracelets will have you braiding in a snap. Get your friends braiding too, and then exchange bracelets!

What You Need:

3 pieces of yarn,
   about 12 inches
   (30 centimeters) long

tape

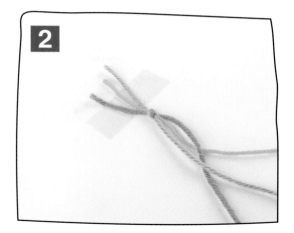

What You Do:

1   Tie the three pieces of yarn together at one end. Tape the knot to a table or other surface.

2   Cross the right string over the middle string. Then cross the left string over the middle string.

3   Repeat until you get to the end of the yarn. Tie the ends of yarn together to finish the braid.

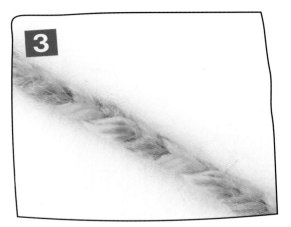

TIP Turn any braid into a friendship bracelet. Simply tie each of the ends together around a friend's wrist.

DRAGON EGG SURPRISE

What can hold an amazing surprise?
A dragon's egg, of course! Your friends
will love this fun-filled egg.

What You Need:

3 pieces of yarn, 48 inches
    (1.2 meters) long
tape
plastic egg
quick-drying glue
toys/candy for inside the egg

What You Do:

1 Braid the three strands of yarn together. Tie the ends in a knot.

2 Wrap the braid around one half of a plastic egg that opens. Use quick-drying glue to hold the braid in place.

3 Repeat steps 2–3 for the other half of the egg.

4 Hide surprises inside the egg.

FEATHER BOOKMARK

Save your spot with these fancy yarn feathers!
Your favorite book will thank you!

What You Need:

yarn

scissors

beads (optional)

What You Do:

1 Cut one piece of yarn as long as your arm. Fold it in half, with the loop facing upward. This will be the middle of the feather.

2 Cut two more pieces of yarn as long as your hand. Fold both pieces in half. Slide one of these loops under the first loop you made so its tails are pointing to the right.

3 Slide the third loop under the second loop and over the first loop. Its tails should point to the left. Pull the left and right tails of yarn tight.

4 Repeat steps 2–3 with more pieces of yarn to make the feather.

5 Trim the edges to create a feather shape.

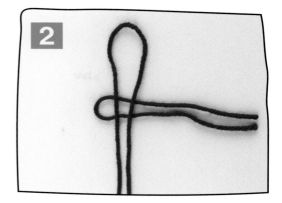

TIP You can make this a zipper pull instead of a bookmark. Add beads to the feathers. Then attach the feather to a zipper with more yarn.

HUG IT!

Don't throw away those plastic drinking straws!
Recycle them and weave a handy hugger for your
water bottle or a mug of hot chocolate!

What You Need:

3 pieces of yarn, about 15 inches (38 cm) long

3 plastic straws

tape

1 piece of yarn, about 30 inches (76 cm) long

button (optional)

What You Do:

1. Thread each of the smaller pieces of yarn through a straw.

2. Tie the yarn in a knot at one end. Tape the straws together below the knot. Tie the end of the long piece of yarn to one of the outside straws.

3. Weave the long piece of yarn in and out of the straws. Stop weaving when you get to the other end of the straws.

4. Remove the tape. Hold the top of the weaving and pull each straw out, one at a time.

5. Tie the tails of the yarn together around a bottle or mug.

TIP Add more straws to make a wider piece. To add a second color, simply tie on a different color of yarn and continue the weave. Glue a button on for an extra touch!

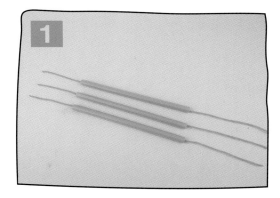

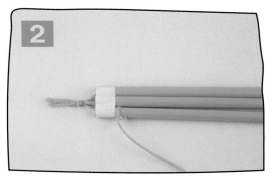

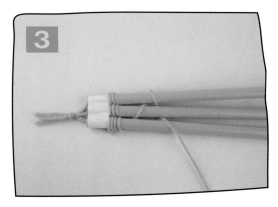

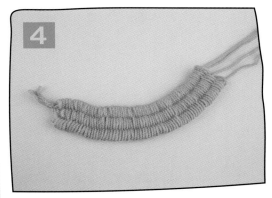

21

MUSTACHE ME!

Ever wanted a fun mustache? You can make your own! You'll laugh out loud at this super simple, super silly mustache.

What You Need:

1 piece of yarn, about 20 inches (51 cm) long

pipe cleaner

additional yarn

scissors

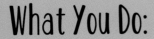

What You Do:

1. Tie the yarn together to make a loop. To test it, put one end around each ear. If it is too short, add more yarn to the loop. If it's too long, tie a knot and make a loop to fit.

2. Set the loop on top of the pipe cleaner.

3. Cut a piece of yarn 10 inches (25 cm) long and fold it in half. Slide the loop under the pipe cleaner.

4. Pull the tails of that piece through the loop. Tug it tight.

5. Cut more pieces of yarn and tie on the same way all they way down the pipe cleaner. Fold over the ends of the pipe cleaner so the wires aren't showing.

6. Bend into a mustache shape and trim the yarn to make different looks. Hook the yarn loops around your ears.

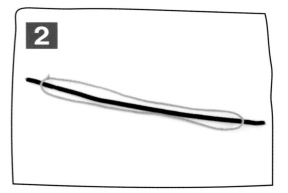

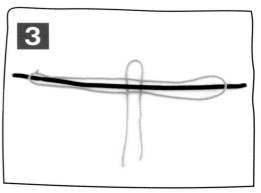

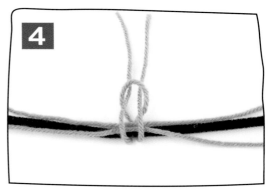

STICK TO IT!

Decorate your locker or room with this
colorful wall hanging. Pick your favorite colors
to brighten up a simple stick. Yarn can turn
anything into a work of art!

What You Need:

scissors

yarn

stick

What You Do:

1 Cut enough pieces of yarn to cover the length of the stick. Fold each piece in half and line them up next to each other.

2 Place the stick across the middle of all the yarn pieces.

3 Bring the tail ends of one piece of yarn through its loop and pull tight. Repeat for the remaining pieces of yarn.

4 Once you've tied all pieces of yarn, trim the ends at an angle or all the same length.

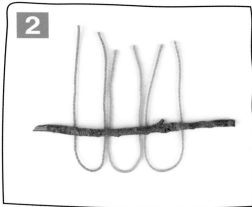

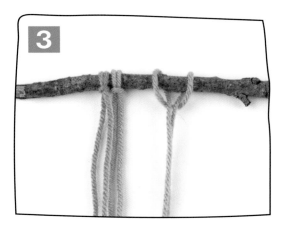

YARN FLOWERPOT

Turn a plain plastic bottle into a flowerpot. Fill it with real plants or make your own. You can even use yarn to make a holder for your new pot.

What You Need:

plastic water bottle

1 piece of yarn, about 25 feet (8 m) long

additional yarn, different color

duct tape/hot glue

key ring (optional)

What You Do:

1 Ask an adult to cut off the spout of the plastic water bottle.

2 Loop the yarn through the spout. Tape or glue one end of the yarn to the inside of the spout.

3 Wrap yarn through and around the spout. To change colors, tie on another piece of yarn and hide the knot inside the spout.

4 Add fake plants to the yarn pot.

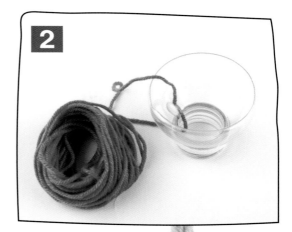

TIP Tie and knot more pieces of yarn to a key ring. Set the yarn pot on the ring and tie knots wherever you'd like. Tie all of the ends together to make a yarn pot holder.

27

CATAPULT

Try launching yarn pom-poms, marshmallows, or even paper balls with this quick and easy catapult. Bombs away!

What You Need:

8 craft sticks

yarn

quick-drying glue

small paper cupcake liner or bottle cap

scissors

plastic lid

small plastic cup

yarn pom-pom

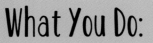

What You Do:

1 Stack six craft sticks together. Wrap them in yarn on both ends.

2 Stack two craft sticks. Wrap them in yarn on one end.

3 Slide the open end of the two-stick stack over the larger stack.

4 Glue a paper liner to the open end of the stack of two sticks.

5 Press down on the stick by the paper liner and let it spring back up. You're ready to launch!

TIP Slide the sticks up or down on the larger stack of sticks to change the projection of your pom-pom.

MOVING TARGET

Make a moving target for your catapult. Cut a hole in the middle of the lid, large enough for a small cup to fit inside. Wrap yarn around the lid and set the target in front of the catapult. Can you get the pom-pom into the cup?

STICK WEAVING

You can use almost anything to make your own loom. Start this project yourself and then make it into a larger piece of artwork for your classroom. Now, that's teamwork!

What You Need:

glue
craft sticks
yarn

What You Do:

1 Glue two craft sticks together to make an X.

2 Start in the middle of the X. Wrap different colors of yarn around the sticks, weaving in and out of the X.

3 To change yarn colors, tie on another piece of yarn.

4 End the weave and tie the yarn tail onto another woven piece in the back.

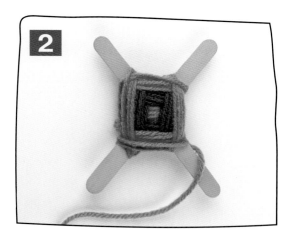

TIP Ask your friends to make a bunch of different stick shapes. Glue or tie the woven shapes together with yarn to make abstract art.

Read More

Hove, Carol. *Make It Yourself!: From Junk to Jewelry*. Minneapolis: Checkerboard Library, an imprint of Abdo, 2018.

Rau, Dana Meachen. *Making Knot Projects*. Ann Arbor, MI: Cherry Lake, 2016.

Uliana, Kim. *Crafting Fun for Kids of All Ages: Pipe Cleaners, Paint, & Pom-Poms Galore, Yarn & String & a Whole Lot More*. New York: Sky Pony Press, 2017.

Internet Sites

The Arts and Crafts Makerspace
http://www.renovatedlearning.com/2014/11/17/the-arts-and-crafts-makerspace/

Easy Peasy and Fun: Yarn Wrapped Carrot Craft for Kids
https://www.easypeasyandfun.com/yarn-wrapped-carrot-craft-for-kids/

Kid Activities: 17 Fun Yarn Crafts for Kids
https://www.kidactivities.net/things-yarn-string/